PROFILES OF FLIGHT

LOCKHEED F-104
STARFIGHTER

PROFILES OF FLIGHT

LOCKHEED F-104
STARFIGHTER
Interceptor/ Strike/ Reconnaissance Fighter

DAVE WINDLE & MARTIN BOWMAN

Pen & Sword
AVIATION

First published in Great Britain in 2011 by
PEN & SWORD AVIATION
An imprint of
Pen & Sword Books Ltd
47 Church Street
Barnsley
South Yorkshire
S70 2AS

ISBN 978 1 84884 449 0

A CIP catalogue record for this book is
available from the British Library

Printed and bound in China
by Printworks Int. Ltd.

Pen & Sword Books Ltd incorporates the Imprints of
Pen & Sword Aviation, Pen & Sword Family History, Pen & Sword Maritime,
Pen & Sword Military, Wharncliffe Local History, Pen & Sword Select,
Pen & Sword Military Classics, Leo Cooper, Remember When,
Seaforth Publishing and Frontline Publishing

For a complete list of Pen & Sword titles please contact
PEN & SWORD BOOKS LIMITED
47 Church Street, Barnsley, South Yorkshire, S70 2AS, England
E-mail: enquiries@pen-and-sword.co.uk
Website: www.pen-and-sword.co.uk

LOCKHEED F-104 STARFIGHTER

No other aircraft in the history of aviation has engendered more controversy or such notoriety and suffered such a high a loss rate over a short period as the Starfighter. Known sometimes as the 'Missile with the Man in It' the F-104 had such stubby little wings that many inferred that it had 'no visible means of support'. Early on the Starfighter was beset with a number of operational problems that resulted mainly from the troublesome General Electric J79-GE-7A engine. By the time the F-104 had logged its 100,000th flight hour, in April 1961, 49 out of 296 Starfighters operated by the USAF had been lost and 18 pilots killed – none of them in combat. From 1958 to early 1963 there were forty serious incidents, which resulted in the deaths of nine pilots and the loss of twenty-four aircraft, and the USAF cut back its F-104 orders. Lockheed's failure to produce F-104s in greater numbers and the loss of so many aircraft looked potentially disastrous for the Burbank, California, company. Yet, within a few years the Starfighter had won a worldwide market with licence production underway in seven countries. Their

XF-104-LO FG-786 (53-7786), the first of two XF-104 single-seat prototypes ordered on 12 March 1953. (Lockheed)

YF-104A FG-955 (55-2955), one of seventeen YF-104As built for service trials with the J79-GE-3 engine. Mach 2 was achieved in an YF-104 on 27 April 1955.
(Lockheed)

governments rushed to buy F-104s in great numbers for their air arms, even when they looked ill suited for the role they were chosen for and when other designs offered more for the same money. But the publication in 1975 of a Lockheed company report revealed that $22 million in 'sales commissions' had been paid to foreign officials, including at least $1 million to Prince Bernhard of the Netherlands. The bribes scandal forced the chairman, vice-chairman and president of the Lockheed Aircraft Corporation to resign. On 1 September 1977 the Lockheed Aircraft Corporation became Lockheed Corporation. F-104 production continued unabated and two years later worldwide Starfighter production ended at 2,577 – 1,241 of them having been built in Europe.

The F-104 originated in May 1952 when Lockheed were offered a contract for the construction of prototypes of a Wright J67-powered, 16-ton interceptor, but the company, whose Advanced Design Group was already working in secret on a much simpler and considerably lighter proposal (the CL-246), declined. In 1951 Hall Hibbard, Lockheed's chief engineer, and Clarence L. 'Kelly' Johnson, assistant chief engineer and chief designer, were determined to create a successful lightweight, uncomplicated jet-fighter design, especially since American fighter pilots in Korea had told Johnson this was what they required. Both men had worked on the P-80, which had been contracted by the USAAF in June 1943 and was completed in just 143 days. After returning from Korea (following a trip in 1951 to see how his F-80 performed), in November 1952 Johnson (named chief engineer at Burbank that same year) began to design a dedicated air superiority fighter, even though at this time, the USAF had no requirement for such an aircraft. Design was carried out at the famous Advanced Development Projects Section or the Lockheed 'Skunk Works' as it was known. This had its origins at the beginning of the P-80 programme when 'Kelly' Johnson, then assistant to Hall Hibbard and chief designer, had housed his ADP (Advanced Development Project) Section in temporary accommodation next to a plastics factory. Its location earned the nickname 'Skunk Works', after the foul-smelling factory in Al Capp's 'Lil Abner' comic strip. (The name stuck and the ADPs later became the Lockheed Advanced Development Company, or LADC, which years later was responsible for building the F-1117A Stealth fighter).

During the development of the F-104, Lockheed drew heavily upon information gleaned during NACA (National Advisory Committee for Aeronautics) wind tunnel tests of the proposed Douglas X-3 Stiletto project, built to investigate the design features of an aircraft suitable for sustained supersonic speeds and which flew on 20 October 1952. Because of adverse drag divergence and pressure shifts at transonic speeds, the Douglas team designed the low-aspect ratio wing for the X-3 with a thickness chord ratio of only 4.5 per cent. The Model 83 (F-104) wing would embody much the same characteristics as the X-3 wing. It would have a sharp leading edge with a thickness ratio of just 3.36 per cent and a maximum thickness of only 4.2 inches adjacent to the fuselage and only 1.96 inches at the tips. At least fourteen completely different designs, including ones with rocket propulsion, wingtip-mounted tail booms, nacelle-retracting landing gear and low-mounted stabilizer were considered before the radical Model 83 design was complete. Considered to be years ahead of its time, it had a long, tapered nose and a short, stubby, unswept, very thin wing, which would encounter little drag. This wing, which the Skunk Works had finally decided upon after first considering delta and swept-wing designs, would extend only 7½ feet from the fuselage and it was angled downwards 10 degrees. The leading edge was so thin it was said that it was sharp enough to cut meat with. Another unique feature was a high T-tail configuration with all-moveable stabilators (stabilizers and elevators), which moved as one unit.

It was believed that the high T-tail posed a hazard in any upward ejection from the aircraft so both XF-104 single-seat tactical fighter prototypes ordered on 12 March 1953 with Wright XJ65-W-6 engines of 7,800lb thrust and 10,200lb with afterburner would be fitted with a Lockheed-built downward-firing rocket-propulsion ejection seat system, the first fully automatic system used on any production fighter aircraft. When these fears proved groundless the Starfighter received an upward-firing rocket-powered Lockheed C-2 ejection seat. Although quoted as 'zero-zero'-capable

YF-104A-11 55-2965 in full 14,800lb afterburner thrust during a night engine run at Edwards AFB, California, in May 1957. (Lockheed)

(zero speed and altitude), a forward speed of at least 98 knots was required for a successful ground level ejection.

The Skunk Works created a very lean and lightweight fighter with a high thrust-to-weight ratio to give it an advantage in the supersonic speed regime in which it would fly and fight. At an all-up weight of just 10,500lb the XF-104 was half the weight of its competitors – the Northrop N-102 Fang, North American NA-212 F-100B (J) Ultra Sabre and the Republic AP-55 Thunderwarrior. Colonel Bruce Holloway at the Pentagon was so impressed with Johnson's proposal, that even though there was no requirement for a design such as the XF-104 he would 'make one!' A list of requirements under Weapon System 303A was drawn up for a pure air superiority day fighter with exceptional climb rate, speed, ceiling, agility and manoeuvrability to supplement and, later replace, the F-100 Super Sabre. General Donald L. Putt (commander USAF Systems Command from 30 June 1953 to 14 April 1954) and General Don Yates concurred and a General Operational Requirement was issued for a lightweight air superiority fighter. One of the major headaches confronting the Skunk Works propulsion engineers was the choice of turbojet for the XF-104. The Allison J71 was projected to

NF-104A-LO 56-0756 zoom-climbing over the Mojave Desert, its Rocketdyne rocket motor at full 6,000lb thrust. (NASA/AFMC History Office)

produce up to 14,000lb thrust, the Pratt & Whitney J75 up to 21,000lb thrust and the General Electric J79, up to 25,000lb thrust, all with afterburning. The J79 offered better specific fuel consumption and lighter dry weight than the two other American engines but it was not expected to be available until early 1956 so Lockheed selected the non-afterburning Wright Aeronautical XJ65-W-6, an Americanized version of the Armstrong-Siddeley Sapphire axial-flow turbojet. This engine, which was built by the Buick Motor Division of the General Motors Corporation, was capable of 7,800lb dry-thrust (later versions developed 10,300lb thrust with afterburning). Lockheed had to design two different airframes because the J65 and J79 each required different engine air inlets and exhaust outlets and the XF-104s were limited in Mach by the inlet temperature of the J65 and J79 power plants.

In January 1953 the Model 83 design was selected under Weapon System WS-303A and on 12 March Lockheed received a Letter Contract for two XF-104-00-LO prototypes (Model 083-92-01). The mock-up was studied and it led to the substitution of a rotary six-barrelled 20mm General Electric M61 30mm Vulcan cannon being mounted in the forward fuselage in place of the two 30mm cannon originally suggested by Lockheed before the mock-up was approved on 30 April.

The end of the Korean War on 27 July 1953 removed the need for a high-performance air superiority fighter from the priority list but subsequent events prompted Lockheed to propose a new career for the Starfighter. Originally, Air Defense Command had anticipated replacing the F-102 Delta Dagger fighter-interceptor with the F-106 Delta Dart by 1954 but the project had been delayed. (The F-106 finally entered service in July 1959.) The XF-104 mission was changed therefore to that of air defence fighter-interceptor with a secondary role as an air superiority fighter. As test pilot Milton O. Thompson once said, the F-104 'was designed only to get to high altitude fast and pass by the enemy at high enough speed to avoid a dogfight and a retaliatory missile. It was never intended to be a dogfighter; instead, it was a greyhound built to nip at the butt of the pit bulls as it passed by'.

In January 1954 the first XF-104 was built in such strict secrecy that there was no official roll-out party. 53-7786 (Company designation 1001) and 53-7787 (Company designation 1002) were taken to the top secret North Base Area at Edwards AFB in the Mojave

Desert where Lockheed Chief Test Pilot, Tony LeVier, and test pilot Herman 'Fish' Salmon flew both prototypes in the test evaluation programme. 53-7786 was used as the aerodynamic test bed while 53-7787 was used to test the armament. Early problems with lateral directional stability revealed a need for a ventral fin. On 28 February 1954, XF-104 53-7786 made an unscheduled short and straight hop before LeVier flew the number one aircraft for the first time on 4 March. 53-7786 experienced undercarriage retraction problems. (This would be rectified later in the YF-104 programme when a forward-retracting undercarriage was installed in place of the rearward-retracting arrangement. (53-7786 was later lost in a crash, on 11 July 1957.)

On 25 March 1955, XF-104-253-7787, now powered by an afterburning Wright J65-W-7 and flown by Lockheed test pilot Ray Goudey, reached a top speed of Mach 1.79 (1,324mph). On 14 April 1955, 53-7787 was lost during a gunnery test flight when 'Fish' Salmon was forced to eject because the ejection seat hatch on the floor blew out. With sudden decompression, Salmon's

NF-104-LO- 56-0760, one of three Starfighters modified in 1963 to be used in the USAF astronaut training programme conducted by the Aerospace Research Pilot School at Edwards AFB, California. (Lockheed)

pressure suit inflated and he could not see what had happened but he believed that he had experienced a gun-firing mishap, as LeVier had done on an earlier flight. (On LeVier's aircraft one of the bolts had blown out of the gun, penetrating a bulkhead and fuel cell aft of the gun bay. The gun bay door also partially opened, allowing fuel from the punctured cell to enter the engine inlet. LeVier had made a flame-out landing on the

lakebed at Edwards AFB. Subsequent investigation of the airframe and gun indicated that high temperatures in the gun bay allowed a round to swell up such that it jammed in the barrel, causing the bolt to blow out when it fired.) Salmon ejected and landed safely.

The XF-104 trials revealed that even with the afterburning version of the J65 turbojet, the production aircraft would not be able to reach design maximum speed. There were also directional stability problems to consider and the need to carry more internal fuel load meant that the nose would have to be lengthened on the next batch of YF-104A service trial aircraft. Despite these problems, on 30 March 1955 the USAF placed an order for seventeen YF-104As to flight-test and evaluate the three early versions of the 14,800lb General Electric YJ79-GE-3, -3A and -3B turbojet series. The YF-104A also differed from the XF-104 by modifications to the air

Four F-104C-5-LOs of the 479th TFW, TAC, on a training mission from George AFB. (Lockheed)

intakes. Later, the equally powerful J79-GE-3A with improved afterburner was standardized. The YF-104A first flew on 17 February 1956. Two months later, on 27 April, it attained Mach 2 for the first time. In August 1956 the seventh YF-104A was transferred to NASA.

Apart from exploring the entire performance envelope and testing the new cannon armament, from April 1956 the YF-104As also would have to test the relatively new AIM-9 (formerly GAR-8) Sidewinder air-to-air heat-seeking missile. Without such armament the Starfighter would be useless in an air defence role. These aircraft (and pre-production F-104As) had the fuselage lengthened from 49ft to 54ft 8in and the tail surfaces were moved aft. Another improvement was the fitting of a variable shock-control semitone, or ramp, in the fuselage-side air intakes to channel the huge amount of secondary airflow at supersonic speed. Also, a brake-chute and an arrestor hook were introduced and a ventral fin positioned level with the afterburner was added to improve stability.

On 27 April 1955 Major Howard C. Johnson powered the XF-104A to Mach 2 for the first time. By the end of 1955 Lockheed had an order for 155 F-104s for Air Defense Command. The first YF-104A was rolled out at Burbank on 23 December 1955 but the appearance of the Starfighter was not made widely known until its first public roll-out on 16 February 1956. The next day the first YF-104A flew, with Herman Salmon at the controls. On 28 February the YF-104A, flown by Joe Ozier, exceeded Mach 2 for the first time. On 2 March 1956 a contract was issued for seven pre-production F-104A series production (fighter-bomber) aircraft very similar to the YF-104A. Lockheed also received authorization for 146 F-104As and six tandem-seat F-104B aircraft for Air Defense Command (a two-seat non-combat-capable (unarmed) trainer version of the F-104A was not proceeded with as the USAF preferred the combat-capable two-seat F-104B) and 56 single-seat F-104Cs for Tactical Air Command. Some 153 F-104A examples were ordered, the last deliveries being made to the USAF in December 1958. Power initially was provided by a General Electric J79-GE-3A of 9,600lb static thrust and 14,800lb with afterburner, but beginning in April 1958, F-104As were retrofitted with the more reliable J79-GE-3B engine. A further retrofit saw the J79-GE-19 of 17,900lb afterburning thrust on some USAF aircraft. Design armament consisted of a 20mm M-61 Vulcan cannon and two AIM-9B Sidewinder AAMs (air-to-air-

air missiles) with AN/ASG-14T-1 fire control system. Unreliability of the early cannon in November 1957 resulted in its removal before the delivery of F-104As to Air Defense Command and the improved M-61A1 cannon was reinstalled in 1964. During operational service use the downward-firing ejection seat was replaced by a Lockheed-designed upward-firing seat (C-2) and standard installation of the ventral fin and flap-blowing system. (The C-2 was used in all F-104s except for those built in Belgium, Germany and the Netherlands. The C-2 was later replaced by the Lockheed S/R-2, which offered true zero-speed, zero-altitude capability, and after 1966 the Martin-Baker Mk GQ7 (F) upward-firing ejection seat was fitted to F-104s built in Belgium, Germany and the Netherlands.) Ten F-104As were given to Pakistan (and were later retrofitted with the J79-GE-11A of 15,800lb maximum thrust); forty-six went to the Republic of China Air Force (RoCAF) on Formosa (Taiwan); and thirty-two were given to Jordan. Four went to NASA from October 1957 to December 1966. One went to Canada as a prototype to initiate the production in this country. In 1960 twenty-four F-104As were modified to QF-104A target drones and three as NF-104 aircraft.

F-104C-5-LO 56-0904 of the 479th TFW, TAC. The single-seat F-104C tactical strike version and two-seat F-104D were developed for use by TAC and deliveries of seventy-seven F-104C aircraft were made. (USAF)

When the Berlin Crisis broke out in summer 1961, all three ANG fighter-interceptor squadrons flying F-104As were activated for deployment to Europe in Operation Brass Wing. *As their range was insufficient for the Atlantic crossing, the F-104As were ferried in Douglas C-124 Globemasters. On 24 November 1961 MATS loadmasters began loading the first F-104A of the recently recalled South Carolina ANG's 157th FIS through the loading ramp of a C-124 to be transported to Morón, Spain. (USAF)*

In June 1958 the USAF had ordered the Northrop T-38 Talon, but when delivery schedules of this dedicated supersonic primary jet trainer slipped it was decided to procure a two-seat, dual-control, combat trainer version of the F-104A as a stop-gap. On 2 March 1956 the USAF placed an initial order for six F-104Bs and on 4 December a contract for twenty additional production F-104Bs was received by Lockheed. To provide space for the second seat, mounted aft beneath an extended canopy, the 20mm Vulcan cannon of the single-seater was removed, some of the electronics were relocated and the internal fuel capacity was reduced. The vertical stabilizer was increased in area by 21 per cent and it featured a power boost rudder. The nose-wheel was re-positioned to the front of the landing gear well and retracted rearward (as on the two XF-104s) instead of forward as on the F-104A. Provision for two underwing and two wingtip-mounted drop tanks was retained. A J79-GE-3A/-3B engine of 9,600lb static thrust and 14,800lb provided power with afterburner. The fin area was increased by 35 per cent and a fully powered rudder was adopted. Armament consisted of just two AIM-9B Sidewinder missiles with AN/ASG-14T-1 fire control system. The first F-104B-1-LO was hand built at Palmdale, California, using a production F-104A airframe and was transported by road to Edwards AFB for its first flight on 16 January 1957. It was used to test the downward-ejection seat initially fitted to all USAF Starfighters and eventually was modified to F-104B production standard. The first production F-104B was delivered to the USAF in September 1957; the last in November 1958. Four F-104Bs were given to the Republic of China Air Force (RoCAF) and eight went to Jordan. In December 1959 an F-104B was given to NASA.

Meanwhile, in November 1954 design work was started on an unarmed photo-reconnaissance version to equip four reconnaissance squadrons in Tactical Air Command (TAC), and in 1955 nineteen RF-104A-LO models were ordered. However, before production began, TAC decided to equip its reconnaissance squadrons with the McDonnell RF-101C Voodoo, which had a longer range and heavier load-carrying capability and in January 1957 all development work on the RF-104A was cancelled. However, on 26 December 1956 Lockheed had received a second order from TAC for an additional twenty-one F-104Cs. TAC looked to the Starfighter because it needed a supersonic tactical strike fighter (fighter-bomber) to replace the North American F-100C Super Sabre and the Republic F-105B Thunderchief had been delayed. The F-104C differed principally from previous versions in having a removable in-flight-refuelling probe fitted on the port side of the fuselage, an all-up AN/ASG-14T fire control system and provision to carry a single Mk 28 nuclear bomb or a Douglas AIR-2 Genie air-to-air rocket. A new J79-GE-7 engine of 10,000lb static thrust and 15,500lb provided power with afterburner. Altogether, seventy-seven F-104C all weather, fighter-bombers were ordered for TAC. The first F-104C flew on 24 July 1958

and TAC accepted the first example on 15 October 1958 during the annual USAF Fighter Weapons Meet at Nellis AFB, Nevada. The last F-104C was delivered in June 1959. From 1958 to early 1963, operational problems, resulting mainly from the troublesome J79-GE-7A engine, caused forty serious incidents, which resulted in the deaths of nine pilots and the loss of twenty-four aircraft. In May 1963 General Electric began a year-long programme called *Seven Up* to modify all existing 7A turbojets. Early in 1963 Project *Grindstone* saw Lockheed modify all remaining F-104Cs to carry two Sidewinders beneath the fuselage, or bombs and

F-104C 56-0894 of Tactical Air Command.
(Brian Allchin)

F-104A-5-LO 56-0737 of the 479th TFW with two wingtip-mounted AIM-9 Sidewinders. (Lockheed)

unguided HE 2.75-inch diameter rockets in pods on underwing and fuselage stations. (This was in addition to the two wingtip-mounted AIM-9 Sidewinders.)

In the 1950s delays and shortcomings had seriously began to afflict the Starfighter programme. Compressor problems with the J79 turbojet caused a slippage in the YF-104A flight-test programme and by early June 1956 doubts about the F-104's ability to fulfil either the interceptor role or any proposed tactical role were emerging because of fuel limitations. Using internal fuel only, the F-104 was reported to have 'an intercept radius of 150 miles against a B-52 type target at 45,000ft'. This

would mean that intercepts at 70,000ft would 'have to be made over the base'.

TAC had a requirement for its F-104Cs to carry the two types of US nuclear payloads or 'special stores' as they were known. One type was the 2,013lb B28 and was designed to be dropped from high altitude at subsonic or supersonic speeds. The other was the 2,195lb B28-1, a parachute-drop bomb, which was designed to be delivered at low altitude under high-g conditions (using the low-altitude bomb system of LABS). These bombs were too big for the Starfighter's weapons bay so each bomb would have to be carried externally as well as the aircraft receiving wingtip and/or underwing auxiliary fuel tanks. It would mean the Starfighter pilot would be denied supersonic performance on any nuclear mission. He might maintain 'operational' speed if he were to discard the fuel tanks en route, but he would then most probably run out of fuel before the target was reached! Since single-seat F-104C aircraft were not yet available – by December 1956 – for the Special Weapon Configuration testing, an F-104A was used for the performance phase and another F-104A for the stability phase. Both F-104As were modified to carry ventral bomb racks to carry the nuclear device. Additional fuel would be carried externally also, in two 165-gallon wingtip tanks and in two 200-gallon underwing pylon mounted tanks.

The Special Weapon Configuration programme, which was carried out over 37 flights totalling 37 hours 30 minutes at Palmdale and at Edwards, revealed serious fuel limitations and a dramatic fall off in the Starfighter's overall speed and distance performance. The tests involving a Starfighter carrying a total of 1,638 gallons of fuel (i.e. with four external fuel tanks in addition to the internal fuel) and a 'special store', reduced the afterburning sea level rate of climb to 23,400ft/min compared with 36,400ft/min for the clean aircraft. Also,

supersonic capability was no longer possible when carrying the five external stores, although about Mach 1.2 could be achieved if the underwing fuel tanks were removed. If the F-104 dropped its external fuel tanks, as they became empty in a typical subsonic strike mission, the nuclear bomb could be delivered onto a target 828 miles from the home base and the aircraft returned safely. It might have been prudent to drop the tanks on any such mission anyway as it was found that the aircraft fish-tailed at speeds above 675 mph lAS (indicated air speed) when any of the external tanks and the nuclear store were carried. Hence, the F-104 pilot would not be able to rely on supersonic performance on any nuclear strike mission. The best he could hope for while carrying the store would be a maximum flight speed using military power of about Mach 0.965 at 20,000ft and Mach 0.945 at 35,000ft. Clearly, the Starfighter would have severe limitations to say the least, if it were used in the nuclear strike role!

By 5 December 1956 it was obvious that though the Starfighter promised spectacular speed and climb performance, there remained a whole host of problems that had to be dealt with. Not least was 'pitch-up' at high angles of attack. This, and delays caused by the need to develop and fit wingtip and underwing tanks, as well as producing an adequate armament system, would 'relegate the early production aircraft to little more than a training role'. And the flight-testing of ten early production F-104As for Phase VI functional development and Phase IV performance and stability tests still had to take place. On 3 November 1956, YF-104A-6 was destroyed in a crash and YF-104A-4 was lost on 15 February 1957. On 1 May 1957 the eighth YF-104A became the fourth test Starfighter to be lost. Lockheed experimental pilot Jack J. 'Suitcase' Simpson ejected upwards, upside down at 17,000ft and lived to tell the tale. On 27 May YF-104A-16 was lost in a crash. A year later, on 6 May 1958, the fourteenth YF-104A was written off. On 26 July 1958 Captain Iven C. Kincheloe was killed in a flying accident at Edwards AFB while piloting F-104A-15 56-772. Kincheloe had received the 1956 Mackay Trophy for setting an altitude record of 126,000ft in the Bell X-2 in September 1956. At the time of his death he was one of three pilots selected to fly the X-15. Altogether, eight service test air vehicles, including the two XF-104s, were destroyed during the period of Starfighter testing, from 1955 to November 1959, and

F-104A-20-LO 56-0769 and 56-0781 of the 83rd FIS from Hamilton AFB, San Francisco, California, in formation over California. (Lockheed)

Two F-104Cs of the 479th TFW assigned to the 8th TFW at Udorn armed with 750lb M117 bombs en route to their target in Vietnam in November 1966. (USAF)

three test pilots were killed in YF-104s when they were forced to eject at low altitude or too near to the ground.

On 26 January 1958 the first batch of F-104As was delivered to Air Defense Command, to the 83rd Fighter Interceptor Squadron (FIS) at Hamilton AFB, California, which became operational on 20 February. Early in 1958 the 83rd FIS also became the first unit to receive the F-104B two-seat trainer version of the Starfighter. However, just three months after going into service the squadron's F-104As were grounded after a succession of accidents caused by compressor stall and flameout of the J79 turbojet engine. The F-104As remained grounded for three months while a new GE-3B engine was installed. During 1958 three other ADC units were equipped with F-104As and F-104Bs. In April the 337th FIS (Fighter Interceptor Squadron) at Westover AFB received its Starfighters and in June, the 538th FIS at Larson AFB, Washington, was also so equipped. In July the 56th FIS at Wright-Patterson AFB, Ohio, became the fourth and final Starfighter squadron in ADC. In October 1958, in Operation *Jonah Able*, twelve F-104As of the 83rd FIS were disassembled, crated and airlifted by USAF Douglas C-124 Globemasters, on temporary deployment to Kungkwan Air Base in Taiwan. (Although a few F-104As had been fitted with an experimental air-refuelling probe, none of the production batch was fitted with the device.) They were needed to augment the forces of General Chiang Kai-shek's Nationalist China's air defence during the Quemoy/Matsu Crisis with the People's Republic of China.

The F-104A had the speed and the altitude to deter an aggressor, but the anticipated early availability of more flexible supersonic fighters and the lack of an all-weather radar capability led to a review of the entire F-104 programme. (Lockheed had tried, unsuccessfully, to install the radar sight system in the needle nose and it had proved totally inadequate in range and power – on a good day it had a radar sight range of between five to ten miles. The type of radar required for a supersonic interceptor capable of Mach 2+, if it was to be effective, was too big and heavy for the F-104.) Deliveries of the Starfighter to Air Defense Command (later Aerospace Defense Command) continued until December 1958 when the final eight F-104As of the 153 built were delivered. That same month the USAF reduced its Starfighter procurement from a total of 722, to just 296

and they were soon phased out to make way for all-weather fighters. Only 153 F-104As were built and just 26 F-104B trainer versions, the first flying on 7 February 1957. Lockheed ultimately produced just 277 F-104A/B/C/Ds for the USAF. (F-104C/Ds were accepted by Tactical Air Command during 1958–1959). F-104As and -Bs equipped the 83rd, 56th and 337th Interceptor Squadrons for less than a year before they were handed over to the 151st, 157th and 197th Squadrons of the Air National Guard (ANG), although later some F-104As, powered by the GE-19 engine, returned to first-line service. Twenty-four F-1C4As were converted to QF-104 target drones, while three were modified to NF-104A models.

In 1959 the US Navy at Navy Weapons Training Center (NWTC) China Lake were loaned three YE-104A/F-104As to test the effectiveness of the AIM-9 Sidewinder air-to-air missile at supersonic speeds. (At this time the Navy was still awaiting delivery of its own high-performance jets such as the Chance Vought F9U Crusader.) Testing using a YF-104A-2 and two F-104As, all of which were crewed by USAF personnel from the 83rd Fighter Interceptor Squadron, began in 1959, although the majority of the Sidewinder missile test firings took place during 1960 and 1961. The YF-104 completed the AIM-9 test programme safely and later became a QF-104A drone but the two F-104As were lost in 1960–61.

During 1960 the F-104As and F-104Bs were phased out of ADC and beginning in February 1960 were transferred to three fighter interceptor squadrons in the ANG. The first was the 157th FIS, South Carolina ANG, at Congaree Air Base. (On 10 November 1961 Congaree was renamed McEntire ANGB in honour of Brigadier General Barnie B. McEntire, the late commander of the South Carolina ANG, who had been killed on 25 May

1961 when he stayed in his crippled F-104A to avoid crashing in a populated area at Harrisburg, Pennsylvania). The 151st FIS, Tennessee ANG, activated at McGhee Tyson Airport, Knoxville, in June and the 197th FIS, Arizona ANG, activated at Skyharbor Airport, Phoenix, in July. Preparation for the mobilization of ANG flying squadrons was still underway when, on 13 August 1961, the Soviets and East Germans began erecting the Berlin Wall. On 1 November all three ANG F-104A fighter interceptor squadrons were activated for deployment to Europe. As their range was insufficient for the Atlantic crossing, the Starfighters were ferried in

F-104C-5-LO 56-0902 of the 436th TFS, 479th TFW, assigned to the 8th TFW at Udorn heads for its target in South Vietnam armed with two 750lb M117 bombs. (USAF)

C-124 Globemasters of the Military Air Transport Service (MATS) in Operation *Brass Wing*. The 157th FIS remained at its home base in South Carolina for the first three weeks of November before relocating to Morôn Air Base in Spain on the 24th. The 151st and 197th Fighter Interceptor Squadrons were based at Ramstein Air Base, West Germany. The 151st assumed alert duty at Ramstein on 19 December. When these three squadrons returned to the USA in August 1962 they once again came under the control of their respective states, although the USAF retained the 197th FIS until September when it was re-equipped with the Boeing C-97G and became a MATS unit.

When the Cuban Missile Crisis erupted on 22 October 1962 the ANG F-104s were returned to duty with Aerospace Defense Command. They equipped the 319th FIS at Homestead AFB, Florida, and the 331st FIS at Webb AFB, Texas, replacing the F-106A and the Convair F-102A respectively The 151st FIS ANG relinquished its F-104As in March 1963 when it converted to the F/TF-102A. The 157th FIS ANG gave

F-104Cs of the 479th TFW at Udorn AB, Thailand. During their tour in South East Asia, the 479th TFW's Starfighters logged 2,269 combat sorties for a total of 8,820 combat hours. (USAF)

up its Starfighters in June 1963 when it re-equipped with the F-102 also. In May 1965 the 331st FIS deployed to Puerto Rico during the Dominican Republic Crisis. All remaining F-104A/Bs were finally phased out of US service when the 319th FIS was deactivated in December 1969. All remaining F-104A/Bs that were serviceable were delivered to Taiwan and to Jordan while all non-serviceable aircraft went into storage at the Aerospace Maintenance and Regeneration Center (AMARC) at Davis-Monthan AFB, Arizona.

On 24 July 1958 the F-104C fighter-bomber variant flew for the first time, with seventy-seven examples being built for Tactical Air Command. The F-104C had a more powerful J79-GE-7A engine, which produced 15,800lb of thrust and was fitted with a probe for in-flight refuelling. It could carry two 170-gallon tanks or two 1,000lb bombs or a Mk 28 special store, or four Sidewinder AAMs. The 'C' was joined on the Burbank production lines by twenty-one tandem-seat F-104D combat trainers, which were also powered by a J79-GE-7A and which could also operate in the ground-attack role. The F-104D combined the cockpit layout of the F-104B with the armament, engine and flight-refuelling capability of the F-104C. Like the B model, it incorporated the larger area vertical fin and its nose landing gear retracted rearwards like that of the F-104B. The first of twenty-one F-104Ds was flight-tested on 31 October 1958 and all were accepted by Tactical Air Command from 1958 to 1959. Beginning in September 1958, the 479th TFW at George AFB, California, was the first to receive the F-104C. In November 1959 the 479th TFW made an overseas deployment to Morôn AB, Spain, where one squadron remained on a rotational basis until 1963. During the 1960 Berlin Crisis the Morôn-based squadron of F-104Cs transferred to Bitburg AB, West Germany, and the three other squadrons at George AFB deployed to Hahn and Ramstein ABs. By early 1962 all except the Morôn-based squadron were back at George AFB and then, when the Cuban Missile Crisis broke out in October 1962, all of the F-1004Cs at George were re-deployed to Key West, Florida. In 1963 a number of F-104Cs of the 479th TFW were employed in operational testing and in November a detachment was sent to the Arctic as part of Project *Diamond Lil*. (A second Arctic deployment was made by the 479th TFW in 1965.)

In 1958–59 the Starfighter achieved considerable fame with a series of outstanding record achievements, becoming the first aircraft to hold World Airspeed and Altitude records simultaneously. On 7 May 1958, Major Howard C. Johnson of the 83rd Fighter Interceptor Squadron attained 91,249ft at Edwards AFB. On 16 May Captain Walter W. Irwin established a world airspeed record of 1,404.19mph over a 15 by 25km course at Edwards. On 18 December 1958, the Starfighter set more records. Flying from NAS Point Magu, California, an F-104A set three time-to-climb records. On 14 December 1959 an F-104C piloted by Captain Joe

Jordan, Edwards AFB test pilot, beat the 1958 Starfighter height record, reaching 103,389ft, making the Starfighter the first aircraft taking off on its own power to exceed the 30,000m (100,000ft) mark. Achieving a top speed of 1,400mph, the F-104C also established a 30,000m time-to-climb mark of 5 minutes 4.92 seconds, which even surpassed the existing balloon record of 101,516ft.

In 1959 Clarence 'Kelly' Johnson received the prestigious Collier Trophy from the American Institute of Aeronautics and Astronautics for his design work on the aircraft. Johnson said:

The large airplane exponents claimed that equal speed, range and fighting power could not be obtained in a smaller airplane because such fixed items as the pilot size, canopy size, engine thrust per square foot of frontal area and fixed equipment item weights, were a smaller percentage of the large airplane weight than of the smaller one. Likewise, the fuselage cross-section and size, in general, would be unfavourable for the smaller airplane, resulting in lower ratios of lift to drag and thrust to drag; even if the same percentage fuel weight could be carried. There was not in existence a small

F-104G DA+243 of JaboG31 *'Boelcke' taxiing in with its drag chute deployed. (GAF)*

engine, which had as good thrust-weight ratios or specific fuel consumption as the larger engines then available. These factors were all true at the time; so it was necessary to make some rather major advances on practically all of these fronts before a successful lightweight fighter could be developed.

Four YF-104As and twenty early production F-104As were modified in 1959–60 by Lockheed in conjunction with the Sperry-Phoenix Company as QF-104A remote-

control target drones. These could be flown by onboard pilots, pilots with remote control from other aircraft and pilots on the ground with radio-control equipment. Initially, six QF-104As were to be maintained for use at Eglin AFB Auxiliary Field Number 3, with the remaining drones to be maintained in storage at Sacramento (the depot responsible for F-104 support) until they were required for use to replace expended drones. (QF-104As were rarely destroyed – each cost $1.7 million – and were normally recovered and used later in testing the Boeing IM-99A and IM-99B Bomarc air defence missile.) The QF-104A was designed to work in conjunction with a DT-33A airborne director aircraft, a mobile ground director station and four Eglin Test Range drone control sites.

Each QF-104A was produced by removing all combat and fire control systems and subsystems and installing radio receivers, transponder beacons, a telemetry transmitting system, an optical scoring system (consisting of five 16mm

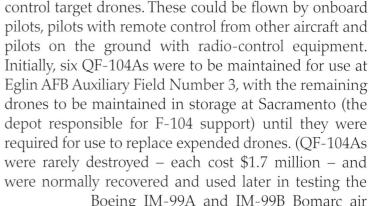

F-104G ZELL DA+102, the second production F-104G, being launched in March 1966. (Via Aeroplane)

cameras), an electronic scoring system, a self-destruct system, a smoke generator, a field arrestor hook and additional fuel tanks in the gun bay area to provide a further 100 gallons of internal fuel capacity. Range was further extended by the continued use of the F-104's wingtip tanks and optional 195-gallon pylon tanks. To permit manned ferry flights by personnel of the 3205th Drone Squadron (DS), a minimum of communications equipment was retained and an upward-firing Lockheed C-2 ejection seat replaced the original downward-firing seat. The first flight of a QF-104A drone occurred in late 1960. Operational use was marred by J79-GE-3A compressor stall problems, landing gear retraction problems and, initially, severe tyre wear on landings. Drone operations finally ended in the early 1970s.

At the 'William Tell 1962 Fighter Weapons Meet', held biennially at Nellis AFB near Las Vegas, a single F-104C, piloted by Captain Charles E Tofferi of the 479th Tactical Fighter Wing at George AFB, beat ten North American F-100 Super Sabres and three Republic F-105 Thunderchiefs. Tofferi championed, 'Thank you one and all for the best airplane I've ever flown. The F-104 really shines. It is so simple to maintain, people with little experience can do it.' Lockheed gleefully announced that:

> The loner generally was regarded as an interloper in the four-day competition, since the 479th was equipped and trained more for nuclear weapons delivery and the contest included several categories in conventional weapons. Captain Tofferi and his F-104C were unstoppable. At the meet's end, he had outscored all other pilots – top marksmen from top TAC units around the world – to post a remarkable victory. He scored 19,018 points out of 24,000 possible. His nearest competitor had 17,304 points. Three of his close-support missions were scored as perfect 1,000s. Downing a towed dart target with his Vulcan 20mm cannon in just 63 seconds he set a new record and picked up the maximum 3,000 points for that division. Among the Starfighter's features, he gave particular credit to its short turning radius (with manoeuvring flaps) and tremendous acceleration for his championship showing.

Despite this, Lockheed generally had little success with several Starfighter projects in the 1960s and 1970s.

An F-104G FN-R of the Royal Norwegian Air Force shadowing a Tupolev Tu-16 'Badger'. (RNWAF)

Although the CL-1200 Lancer proposal, made in 1961, as a concept for the lightweight fighter of the 1980s and 1990s, at one time looked as if it would be a success the aircraft finally lost out to the Northrop F-5E Tiger II in November 1970 and the Lancer never entered production. The Lancer was a Lockheed Skunk Works second-generation project derived from the F-104 with the same fuselage but with new, shoulder-mounted wings of increased area and its tailplane moved from the tip of the vertical and relocated to the base of the aft fuselage. A more powerful Pratt & Whitney TF30-PW-100 or F100-PW-100 turbofan engine was chosen to power the new Starfighter. The gross weight was estimated at 35,000lb or 17.5 tons and the top speed at

1,700 mph at 35,000ft. In 1970 the USAF wanted to acquire a number of CL-1200s for use as high-performance-engine test aircraft and planned to procure one experimental Lancer, to be designated X-27. Similar to the CL-1200, the X-27, however, featured modified engine air inlets of rectangular shape. The X-27 programme was terminated through lack of funding before any aircraft could he built.

The F-104/VTOL (vertical take-off and landing) project was first proposed in 1962. It would have seen the F-104G fitted with wingtip lift engine pods, Rolls-Royce RB.181 lift engines and a fuselage-mounted RB.168R main propulsion engine. Lockheed, Short Brothers and Harland of Belfast (who had pioneered VTOL with its 'flying bedstead' project) discussed the proposal in which the wingtip pods were to contain seven vertically mounted lift engines with detachable fuel tanks fore and aft of the stainless steel power plant bay. Each lift engine was to have a forward-facing inlet

door that would adjust automatically for different airflow conditions. Swivel nozzles were to direct airflow downwards from the pods through a 15-degree arc on either side of the vertical thrust line. By deflecting the nozzles simultaneously, the pilot would be able to control fore and aft movements while hovering. They would also be used, by differential deflection, for yaw control. Pitch control would be achieved by varying pitch settings between the four forward and three rear

An F-104G of the Royal Norwegian Air Force shadowing a Tupolev Tu-114 'Moss'. (RNWAF)

lift engines and through a pitch-control vane installed in the main engine exhaust system. The F-104G/VTOL programme never reached production because, apart from the exceptionally high cost of fuel needed to blast the Starfighter off the ground, the advanced nature of the true-VTOL aircraft, the British Hawker P1127 Kestrel, made the F-100/VTOL virtually redundant at birth. (The P1127 design, which was evaluated by the tripartite squadron consisting of US, RAF and *Luftwaffe* pilots, ultimately led to the highly successful Harrier VTOL jet.) A larger-wing F-104 development was also proposed as an alternative to the MRCA (Multi Role Combat Aircraft) then being designed as a multinational European project.

In the early 1960s the Zero-Length-Launch, or ZELL, programme was conducted in great secrecy at Edwards AFB on the second production F-104G, after the *Luftwaffe* had identified a need to launch their F-104s from no-runway areas in Europe. The aircraft was structurally modified to accept an RS B-202 rocket booster manufactured by Rocketdyne, which developed 65,000lb of thrust for 7.9 seconds. Twelve dummy and eight piloted launches were carried out in two phases during 14 December 1962 to 28 August 1963 and 18

March to 22 July 1964. Eight piloted launches were accomplished with amazingly few problems and a follow-on programme involving several additional launches was conducted in Germany. The final report contained the statement 'Zero-length launches of the F-104 aircraft have been demonstrated to be entirely feasible'.

The F-104H was a 1964 Lockheed-proposed simplified single-seat version of the TF-104G for export with an optical gunsight in place of the Autonetics F15A NASARR fire-control system and able to carry out both the interceptor and strike roles. Although offered to Saudi Arabia, the F-104H lost out to the English Electric Lightning and no F-104H models were built.

For almost twenty-two years, until 21 April 1978, the National Advisory Committee for Aeronautics (NACA), which became the National Air and Space Administration (NASA) on 1 October 1958, operated fourteen Starfighters of various descriptions on a variety of tasks in support of NACA/NASA space research projects. In 1962 Lockheed received a contract from the USAF Air Research and Development Command to modify three F-104As to NF-104A Aerospace Trainer Aircraft configuration. These were for training candidate

Two F-104Gs of the Royal Norwegian Air Force over Norway. (RNWAF)

astronauts at the USAF Aerospace Research Pilots School (ARPS) at Edwards AFB, California, which was commanded by famed aviator, Colonel Charles E. 'Chuck' Yeager. The three NF-104As, which had an empty weight of 13,400lb and a gross take-off weight of 21,800lb, and which were delivered to Edwards from October to November 1963, were to be used as test beds for flights above the atmosphere to familiarize pilots with zero-g and the use of reaction control systems such as found on the Bell X-15. Simulated training using the NF-104As involved a much lower operating cost than using three X-15 aircraft. In order to attain altitudes at which the reaction control system would function, a Rocketdyne LR121/AR-2-NA-1 liquid fuel auxiliary rocket engine of 6,000lb thrust was mounted at the base of the fin above the jet pipe of the J79-GE-3B turbojet, which was retained. The rocket engine, which used JP-4 and hydrogen peroxide, was throttle controlled from 3,000 to 6,000lb thrust with approximately 1 minute 45 seconds' burn time. The original tail fin was replaced with the larger fin as fitted to the TF-104G. The wingspan was increased by 4ft to 25.94ft and a metal nose cone replaced the plastic one. All non-essential equipment, including the Vulcan cannon, AN/ARC-66 UHF radio, AN/ASG-14T-1 fire control system, ILS (Instrument Landing System), braking parachute and auxiliary wingtip tanks, were deleted. The wingtips were extended 2ft and the engine air inlet shock half-cones, modified.

To enable the astronauts to get the feel of the hydrogen peroxide controls with which they would steer their spacecraft, each NF-104A was provided with control thrusters at the nose, tail and wingtips. Reaction control thrusters were added in the test nose boom with pitch and yaw vanes and on the wingtips for roll control.

A separate 'stick' controller was installed on the instrument panel for the reaction control system. A three-axis reaction control damper system was also added, sharing the thrusters with those of the primary control system. These systems also used hydrogen peroxide for fuel. Internal tanks were added for the peroxide. A nitrogen-pressurized cockpit was also installed. The typical mission profile for the NF-104A involved a level acceleration at 35,000ft to Mach 1.9, ignition of the rocket motor at nearly full-rated thrust, starting a shallow climb while continuing to accelerate to Mach 2.1, and a rapid 3.5g pull-up into a steep climb at 50–70° pitch altitude. The J79 afterburner would

TF-104G 12663 of the Royal Norwegian Air Force. (RNWAF)

normally blow out at about 70,000ft, followed by the main engine at 80,000ft. The rocket motor continued to run until fuel starvation (about two minutes' total). At this point the aircraft was well over 100,000ft and reaction controls were exercised to affect a pushover and re-entry manoeuvre. J79 restart was initiated from 40,000 to 35,000ft and, following restart, return to base. It was standard practice upon return from a flight above the stratosphere to conduct a precautionary simulated flame-out approach to landing. The test programme consisted of forty-two flights from 9 July to 29 October, the average duration of which was thirty-four minutes due to the mission profile.

On 15 November 1963, Major Robert W. Smith piloted 56-0756 to 22.5 miles (118,860ft) to record an unofficial world altitude record from a ground take-off at Edwards AFB. On 6 December 1963, 56-0756 reached 120,800ft. On the morning of 12 December 1963 Chuck Yeager flew 56-0760 to 108,000ft. In the afternoon he let the rocket motor carry him over the top at 104,000ft before the stabilizer froze into the climb position and the NF-104 fell off flat and went into a spin. The Starfighter made fourteen flat spins from 104,000ft until impact on the desert floor. Yeager stayed with the aircraft

through thirteen of these spins before he ejected safely at 8,000ft. Yeager survived but he was hospitalized for a month while surgeons treated his severely burned face and hands. He also lost the tips of two of his fingers after using a knife to cut off a burning glove.

A second NF-104A was lost in 1963. The third and final loss of a NASA F-104 was on 8 June 1966 when Joe Walker flew F-104N (013) as part of a formation of aircraft that were powered by General Electric engines. The other aircraft – all provided by the Flight Test Center – were the No. 2 North American XB-70A Valkyrie, piloted by Alvin S. White, the North American test pilot, and Major Carl C. Cross, a US Navy F-4B Phantom, a YF-5A and a T-38 Talon. Clay Lacy, the famous aerial photographer, was hired by General Electric to photograph the formation from a Learjet. The formation, consisting of the F-104N and YF-5A off the Valkyrie's right wing and the T-38 and the F-5B off the left, flew a racetrack pattern around Edwards . Suddenly, Walker's F-104N pitched up and rolled to the left, towards the Valkyrie. 013 continued up and over the XB- 70A's wing, colliding with the twin vertical tails, severely damaging the right tail and tearing off the left tail. The Starfighter broke in two and exploded in a ball

F-104Gs of the Luftwaffe. *(GAF)*

*RCAF CF-104 12797 in formation
with Canadair Sabre Mk 6 of 412
'Falcon' Squadron. (CAF)*

of flames following the collision and burned as it fell towards the Mojave Desert. Walker had no time to eject and was found dead in the cockpit still strapped to his seat. The XB-70A flew on for sixteen seconds then suddenly rolled off to the right and appeared to enter a spin, finally impacting in the desert twelve miles north of Barstow. White managed to eject after some initial difficulty with his escape capsule. Cross died in the aircraft cockpit.

The three NF-104As were followed by eleven F-104Ns, which were primarily used as supersonic chase planes. During the period 27 August 1956 to 21 April 1978 at least nineteen different pilots flew the Starfighter during its NACA/NASA career. Included in this total are Apollo astronauts and X-1S, lifting-body, XB-70A Valkyrie and YF-12 pilots. In 1986 ten F-104s remained. (In June 1971 NF-104A 56-0762 suffered an explosion at Mach 1.15 while at 35,000ft when hydrogen peroxide leaked into the Starfighter's rear fuselage. Captain Howard C. Thompson managed to land the aircraft safely but it had lost half its rudder and rocket motor.) These were still being used as chase and research aircraft, notably as part of the NASA High Alpha Flight Research Program, together with McDonnell Douglas F-18s, which subsequently replaced the Starfighter at Edwards. The last two F-104s were retired by NASA on 3 February 1994. The last flight was made the following day, bringing to an end more than 37 years and more than 18,200 F-104 Starfighter flights.

In April 1965 twenty-five F-104Cs of the 436th TFS, 479th TFW, were dispatched to Da Nang AB, South Vietnam to fly MiG combat air patrol (MiGCAP) missions. Detachments were also sent to Kung Kuan, Taiwan. To protect strike aircraft from the MiGs of the NVNAF, the F-104Cs were armed with their single M61A1 20mm Vulcan cannon and four AIM-9 Sidewinder air-to-air missiles. On the night of 20 September 1965, Major Philip E. Smith tried to relieve another F-104C pilot who had been flying a MiGCAP on station over the Gulf of Tonkin in bad weather. Smith's navigation system failed and he was forced to seek lower altitude in an effort to establish his position. Instead, two People's Republic of China F-6 (MiG-19) fighters intercepted Smith. One of these, piloted by Gao Xiang, destroyed the Starfighter at low altitude over Hainan Island with cannon fire. Meanwhile, two other F-104Cs, who were flying RESCAP (Rescue Combat Air

Patrol) this night, had tried unsuccessfully for two hours to find Major Smith. Returning to Da Nang, they had a mid-air collision and both pilots were killed. Smith, meanwhile, had ejected safely but had been captured and taken prisoner. Smith, who was the only F-104 pilot in South East Asia to be shot down and captured, was held in China until his release in 1973. A week after the loss of the three F-104Cs, a fourth Starfighter was lost in Vietnam when it was shot down by anti-aircraft fire. F-104Cs (and Northrop F-5As) did not possess the range and carried too few weapons for the MiGCAP mission and the McDonnell F-4C Phantom II soon

assumed this role. In November 1965 the remaining F-104Cs of the 436th TFS were rotated back to George AFB, California. In Vietnam the Starfighter had flown some 506 combat sorties, totalling 1,706.9 combat hours, with the loss of four F-104Cs.

Beginning in May 1966 the first F-104Cs of the 479th TFW were sent to South East Asia, to be based at Udorn Royal Thai Air Force Base (RTAFB) in Thailand where they came under the control of the 8th TFW. This time the F-104Cs, which by now were camouflaged, flew low-level, close-support strikes against North Vietnamese lines of communication. By June 1967 all

F-104G D-8145 of 306 Squadron of the Royal Netherlands Air Force. (Dutch Defence Dept)

Three F-104Gs of 350ème/1 Wing de Chasse/1 Jachtwing of the Belgian Air Force. (FAé/BLu)

four squadrons were in action but the Starfighter's short range, even with in-flight refuelling, was insufficient for the majority of missions in South East Asia, and in July the 479th TFW was rotated back to George AFB for the last time. They were replaced in South East Asia by the F-4D Phantom. In thirteen months the F-104Cs had flown a total of 2,269 combat sorties, totalling 8,820 combat hours. Losses now totalled eight Starfighters missing in action (two to Soviet-built SA-2 surface-to-air (SAM) missiles and six to AAA) and another six were destroyed in operational accidents. In the summer of 1967 the surviving F-104C/Ds in the USAF inventory were transferred to the 198th TFS of the Puerto Rico ANG where they replaced the F-86H Sabre. This unit operated Starfighters until its conversion to the LTV A-7D Corsair II in the summer of 1975 and the last Starfighter in USAF service was phased out of operational service in 1975, although they continued to be used in a training role until 1983.

When ADC and TAC withdrew the F-104 from its inventories in the early 1960s, the Starfighter story might have ended. However, on 18 March 1959 *Herr* Franz-Josef Strauss, the Federal German defence minister, signed a contract for ninety-six Starfighters. It was an incredible decision given that the Starfighter was still unproven as a multi-mission aircraft but in *Luftwaffe* service the thirty F-104F two-seat trainers (identical to the F-104D) and sixty-six F-104G multi-role, all-weather fighters were to replace the F-84F Thunderstreak in the strike role, the F-86 Sabre in the air defence role and the RF-84F Thunderflash in photo-reconnaissance. The F-104G would also be standard equipment in the *Marineflieger*, even though the German Navy preferred the British Hawker Siddeley Buccaneer, which was considered a superior aircraft in this role, especially for low-level offshore sorties. The F-104G differed from the F-104C principally in having a reinforced structure, larger tail surface area with fully powered rudder (as used on the two-seater), combat manoeuvring flaps, vastly improved electronics centred around the Autonetics F15A NASARR and a larger capacity for weapons loads. The Vulcan cannon of the earlier versions was retained but additional attachments to take up to four Sidewinder missiles were fitted. Also, the NASARR system provided radar search, acquisition and automatic tracking for lead-collision or lead-pursuit attack with missiles. A director-type gunsight was used for the cannon, giving optical indication of line of sight, with the lead angle furnished by the Autonetics Fl5A NASARR computer. The bombing computer was linked with the inertial navigator, the air-data computer and the NASARR fire control system. The F-104G (a Lockheed-built model) was flown on 7 June 1960 and the first Canadair-built version followed in July 1963. The Canadian-built F-104G differed from European manufactured models, principally in having the F-15AM-11 NASARR, which was optimized for both the air-to-air and air-to-ground roles and a J79-GE-Il engine of 10,000lb static thrust and 15,800lb with afterburner. European-built aircraft were powered with engines co-produced under licence by MAN-Turbo in

Germany, the Fabrique Nationale in Belgium and FIAT in Italy.

Early in 1960 German pilot training began with Lockheed's 'Conversion flight F-104F' course at Palmdale and American instructors trained German F-104 personnel at Luke AFB, Arizona, using thirty F-104F trainers. From 1962 to 1964 the 479th TFW also trained German Starfighter pilots on the F-104D at George AFB, California. In October 1959 the first F-104F was handed over to German military officials. Wartime fighter ace Günther Rall who became the first of over 2,000 German Starfighter pilots was the first student to solo, on 24 February 1960. In April a training school at Nörvenich was established. After the first German ground crews had been trained in the United States, ground crew training was carried out in Germany at Kaufbeuren. Since not enough F-104Fs were available to satisfy all the training needs, Belgian, Dutch and Italian Starfighter

CAF CF-104 104810 with practice bomb dispenser on the centre-line. (CAF)

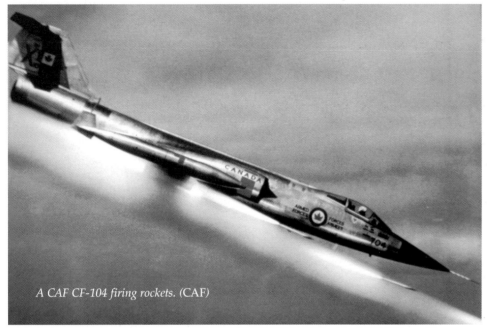

A CAF CF-104 firing rockets. (CAF)

a few F-104G models remained in the United States for pilot training by 1962. These aircraft were also used in the Multinational 'Joint Test Force' at Edwards AFB for evaluating the sub-system (autopilot and navigation system and so on) before the F-104Gs were shipped to Germany.

In October 1962 the first TF-104G two-seat advanced combat trainer version of the F-104G was flown. The TF-104Gs were combat-ready aircraft fitted with NASARR radar and underwing racks for carrying stores. Including forty-eight TF-104G aircraft with components manufactured by the European consortiums, Lockheed built a total of 220 TF-104Gs in six versions for MAP delivery to the *Luftwaffe* and the Italian Air Force, as well as for direct delivery to the Royal Netherlands Air Force, the *Luftwaffe* and the Belgian AF and the Italian Air Force. Germany received 136 TF-104Gs from Lockheed, 30 of which were retained in the US where they were used at Luke AFB, Arizona, for training *Luftwaffe* pilots. Both the

pilots were also trained by the *Luftwaffe*. In August 1961 the first F-104Gs built by Lockheed were handed over to the *Bundeswehr*. In December 1961 the first F-104G built under licence was completed and handed over to the *Luftwaffe*. In all, Germany eventually received a total of 916 Starfighters acquired for the *Luftwaffe* and *Marineflieger*, 652 of them licence-built in Europe. Only autopilot and the Vulcan cannon were deleted, as was the centreline rack for the nuclear store. Fuel tanks and avionics were relocated to make room for the additional cockpit. Altogether, 104 TF-104Gs were built for the *Luftwaffe* and the *Marinefliegerdivision* (Navy Flying Division) of the *Bundesmarine* (Federal Navy).

An all-weather, day and night photographic reconnaissance version of the TF-104G fitted with cameras, infra-red and sideways-looking (SLAR) radar was proposed for use by the *Luftwaffe* but the McDonnell RF-4E Phantom II was chosen instead for the reconnaissance mission.

Two *Marinefliegergeschwadern* (MFG/wings) – MFG1 and MFG2 – began re-equipping with the F-104G in the spring of 1963. From 1964 onwards they replaced Hawker Sea Hawks in the anti-shipping role in the Baltic, where they successfully operated on strike/attack and reconnaissance until 1986. From 1977 their Starfighters were armed with a pair of MBB Kormoran anti-shipping missiles in place of the French AS30 missiles. The Kormoran gave the Starfighter the ability to fire at enemy shipping from a distance of 18.6 miles. The *Marineflieger* received additional ex-*Luftwaffe* F-104Gs and RF-104Gs when the tactical

reconnaissance units replaced the latter with the RF-4E Phantom from 1971 to replace those Starfighters lost in accidents. The RF-104G was almost identical to the F-104G except for the removal of guns and the adoption of photographic equipment. Lockheed built 40 RF-104G examples; the North Group (Fokker) 119 and the Italian Group (FIAT-Aeritalia) 30. Aircraft for the KLu (Royal Netherlands Air Force) had an external ventral camera pack, while the majority of the others carried three KS-67A cameras in the forward fuselage. In both cases the M61 cannon and its 725-round magazine aft of the cockpit were removed to make room. Many RF-104Gs were subsequently modified to F-104G standard.

All told, by April 1989, the *Luftwaffe* and *Marineflieger* combined had lost, or had written off, 292 Starfighters, with 120 pilots and crew killed. Most *Luftwaffe* and *Bundesmarine* F-104Gs were later retrofitted with the updated, German-built J79-MTU-JIK engine. From 1967 onwards the Lockheed C-2 upward-firing ejection seat as originally fitted was phased out in favour of the Martin-Baker GQ7(F) 'zero-zero' seat. The 1,127th and last F-104G was delivered by MBB in 1973. In all, the *Marineflieger* received 119 F-104Gs and 27 RF-104Gs. MFG1 operated the F-104G from 1964 to 1 July 1982,

Royal Danish Air Force F-104G R-756 of ESK 723 in 1980. (Author's coll.)

while MFG2 operated the Starfighter from 1965 to the summer of 1986; both wings converting to the Panavia Tornado IDS (interdiction, strike, anti-ship).

All the F-104Cs had been withdrawn from use in December 1971. At its peak in the mid-1970s the Starfighter equipped five nuclear-armed *Jagdbombergeschwadern* (Tactical Support units), two *Jagdgeschwadern* (Interceptor units) and two *Aufklärungsgeschwadern* (Tactical Photo-reconnaissance units). Starfighter phase-out began in 1971 and *JaboG34* was the last Starfighter operational unit when it finally retired the F-104G in October 1987.

Lockheed knew that where West Germany led, the other nations would follow and NATO nations queued up to buy the new wonder plane in great numbers. On 2 July 1959 Canada announced that the Canadair-built

CF-104 had been selected to replace the Canadair Sabre Mk 6 and the Avro Canada CF-100 Canuck in the eight squadrons of the 1st Air Division, RCAF, in France and Germany. Some 340 (CL-90) Starfighters were built under licence by Canadair, with the Orenda-built J79-OEL-7 engine of 10,000lb static thrust and 15,800lb with afterburner. The first 200 aircraft were built under a licence agreement from Lockheed on 24 July 1959. Externally, these aircraft were little different from the F-104G. They retained provision for the removable refuelling probe as fitted to USAF Starfighters, but the R24A NASARR was optimized for the air-to-air role and the Vulcan cannon was removed and replaced by additional fuel tanks. Other equipment was as specified by the RCAF. Twenty-two CF-104D two-seat advanced trainers and sixteen two-seat advanced trainers were built by Lockheed for the RCAF. All were powered by the Orenda-built J79-OEL-7 engine.

The introduction of the CF-104 Starfighter marked a change of role from air defence to nuclear strike. Operating in the strike role, the CF-104 carried a single

F-104DJ trainers and F-104J single-seat models await delivery to the Japanese Self-Defence Force in the pre-flight hangar at the Mitsubishi Heavy Industries' Komaki plant near Nagoya. (Lockheed)

high-yield tactical nuclear weapon on the centre-line. This weapon could have been delivered using a LABS (low-altitude bombing system) toss manoeuvre, or in a low-level laydown attack. Ultimately, the RCAF (Canadian Armed Forces from 28 February 1968) received 238 CF-104/-104Ds. On 5 February 1964 French bases had to be evacuated following the French–US disagreement on the storage of nuclear weapons and the CAF Starfighter squadrons relocated to bases in Baden-Söllingen and Zweibrücken in West Germany. After the Canadian government's rejection of the nuclear role in 1968, CF-104s were assigned to conventional ground attack and in 1974 the M-61 cannon was installed.

Lieutenant Colonel David L. Bashow, a Canadian CF-104 pilot, recalls:

It was the most beautiful aircraft to ever grace the skies. The durable love affair started in the early 1960s when I first saw this striking machine with its pencil-thin fuselage and tiny canard-like wings and was consummated in 1972 when I first flew the jet. It endures to this day, nearly 2,400 flight hours later. The Americans and Germans liked to call the F-104 the 'Zipper' or the 'Zip'. We would occasionally refer to it in jest as 'the aluminium death tube', or 'the Flying Phallus', but more often than not, we would just call it 'the 104' or by its given name, 'the Starfighter'. Somehow it seemed so appropriate – an elegant name for an elegant aircraft. I *never* heard anyone in the pilot community call it 'the missile with the man in it'. That was pure press hype. Perhaps more to the point, I never heard a pilot call it 'the widow maker' and I don't know a self-respecting 104 pilot who would. This is because none of us who flew her blamed her for the relatively high accident rate incurred during 104 operations, especially during the early transition days. For the most part, the demanding role of the 104 in NATO was the main reason for the elevated accident rate, not the aircraft itself. Unfortunately, the 104 garnered a reputation over time as a 'killer' aircraft. In fact, it was an extremely honest aircraft and as long as it was flown within the boundaries of its flight envelope and was treated with respect, it was utterly dependable. The Canadian accident rate is comparable to that of the other NATO members who operated the 104. Although 113 of the 238 CF-104s produced were destroyed in

F-104J 46-8692 of the Japanese Self-Defence Force.
(Lockheed)

accidents during its Canadian service, it must be remembered that this record represents 25 years of continuous service in a very demanding environment. Thirty-seven Canadian pilots forfeited their lives on CF-104 operations. Needless to say, this record says a great deal for the escape system of the aircraft and there were a great many successful ejections, even in marginal conditions. The biggest accident cause factor was the role to which the jet was exposed – the high-speed, low-level arena where opportunities to err are legion.

Since the jet was only equipped with one engine, if you lost that engine at low altitude, you were in a world of hurt … It wasn't a devious airplane. It just demanded respect and punishment for a major transgression was often swift and fatal. By and large, 104s did not kill pilots. Pilots killed pilots and 104s. In the spring of 1986, the Canadian Armed Forces retired the Starfighter from its inventory.

MBB, Fokker-Aviolandia, SABCA-Fairey, FIAT and Canadair built 1,127 F-104Gs. On 20 April 1960 the Netherlands placed an initial order for Starfighters and

CF-104 104895 firing rockets over the Cold Lake flying area of Canada.
(Andy Graham via Stephen Fochuk)

Belgium followed on 20 June. Altogether, the *Koninklijke Luchtmacht* (KLu, Royal Netherlands Air Force) received 138 Starfighters (18 RF-104Gs, 102 F-104Gs – including 25 F-104Gs built by FIAT – and 18 Lockheed/co-produced TF-104Gs). The first Starfighter to be assembled by Fokker flew on 11 November 1961 and the first Fokker-built Starfighters were delivered to the KLu on 12 December 1962 where they entered service with 306 (Reconnaissance) Squadron, which was in the process of replacing its Hawker Hunters and F-86K Sabres. It became the Starfighter *Operationele Cortversie Unit* (OCU), also known as the *Dutch Masters*. In July 1964, 306 Squadron became fully operational on the RF-104G. The RNLAF lost forty-four Starfighters and nineteen pilots killed, operating F-104Gs in the fighter-bomber role until 1984 when re-equipped with the F-16. The last Starfighter was withdrawn from service in November 1984.

Beginning in February 1963, the *Force Aérienne Belge* (BAé)/ *Belgische Luchtmacht* BLu) received 100 SABCA-built F-104Gs and twelve Lockheed-built TF-104Gs. Belgium retired the last of their F-104s in September 1983. Jan Govaerts, a 2,500-hour veteran Belgian Air Force F-104 pilot recalls:

No matter what you call her the F-104 was quite an aircraft! A mistress, a temptress, she could lure the Belgian Starfighter pilots from a warm hearth, soft arms, hobbies, weekends and even holidays, if she was 'available' to be flown. All through the years the Starfighter acquired for itself the nickname 'widow maker'. In West Germany *Inspektor-General* Johannes Steinhoff of the *Luftwaffe* called the 104 'a most exceptional aircraft'. [Steinhoff also said that 'The Starfighter was forever jealous of the pilot's attention. It rewarded discipline with deeds of airmanship; it could punish the dilatory or those who gave themselves to distractions. It was a marvel in capable hands and merciless to the careless.'] Germany, one of the great users of the plane, put 916 Starfighters into the line, but lost 270 of them in crashes, killing 110 pilots. A sorrowful record but they were not alone. [Belgium lost forty F-104s and twenty-three pilots killed.] Whatever she was called or whatever people thought of her, depended on what colleagues were flying. Mirage pilots regarded the F-104 Starfighter with disdain. Some of the Training Command instructors thought that to be threatened with a tour on F-104s was

F-104Gs of MFG2 of the German Marineflieger *in January 1989.*
(Marineflieger)

SABCA-built F-104G FX-99 of the Belgian Air Force now displayed at Canadian Warplane Heritage at Hamilton, Ontario. (Lockheed)

worse than being assigned to the salt mines.

The good old 379 was a marvellous engine powering the Starfighter like a rocket. With the afterburner going and with very little fuel remaining, you could really put the 104 on its tail and zoom it up. As far as I know the Belgian Air Force never experienced an airborne engine failure. To take off we had to go full forward on the afterburner and this is where the fun started. There was only one way to light the afterburner and that was the good way! With the pilot burner blazing in the exhaust the afterburner had to light and give you the 'kick in the ass', if you set the throttle position correctly! If not, the nozzle opened and instead of having thrust, it gave you the impression of slowing down! Sometimes, it confused pilots so much that they aborted take-off. Sometimes they returned and said, 'This aircraft does not go into the afterburning range properly.'

The F-104 was not an ideal dog-fighter. Moreover it was a 'hit-and-run' fighter, which was due to its tremendous climbing speed and ability to accelerate to whatever speed was needed. This does not mean that as a fighter pilot you were unable to defend yourself against an aggressor. 'Air Combat manoeuvring' held no secrets for us in 1 Wing at Beauvechain, but there were limits. One of these limitations was the ultimate angle of attack where the aircraft is no longer able to respond and flips over in the 'pitch-up' attitude, followed by a difficult-to-control spin. The book even said: 'A spin revolution will result in a loss of about 1,800–2,000ft with each revolution raking five to six seconds and producing rate of descent of approximately 18,000ft per minute. The aircraft should be abandoned if rotation has not stopped by 15,000ft AGL!

On 2 March 1961 Italy had signed a licence production contract to build 155 F-104Gs. The *Aeronautica Militare Italiana* (AMI) received a total of 124 FIAT-built F-104Gs with which to equip its Starfighter *gruppi* (squadrons). In turn, twenty-four TF-104Gs (twelve Lockheed built and twelve co-produced) were also received by the AMI. The F-104G became operational in March 1963. Beginning in February 1970, the F/RF-104Gs were supplemented by the introduction of the much-improved F-104S *caccia ogni tempo* (all-weather interceptor) version produced in Italy for the AMI for interception and interdiction/strike duties (and for Turkey for interception). On the F-104S the M-61 20mm cannon and its ammunition can were deleted and replaced by the Raytheon Sparrow missile control/CW radar system. Two new wing stores stations and pylons at BL104 were added to take two underwing Raytheon AIM-7 Sparrow III radar-seeking missiles and/or two AIM-9 Sidewinder missiles. Also, fuselage-mounted stores stations at BL22 were incorporated and the F-15A NASARR radar was upgraded to the R-21G configuration and the Raytheon system was integrated with it. The additional hard-points gave the F-104 a total of nine: one at the fuselage centre-line, two at fuselage BL22, four wing pylon stations at BL75 and BL104 and two at the wingtips. The increase in weight and a need to improve overall performance led to the adoption of the J79-GE-19 of 11,870lb static thrust and 17,900lb with afterburner. As well as the two FIAT-built F-104Gs modified to F-104S standard by Lockheed, the AMI received 204 FIAT-built examples.

Deliveries of the F-104S ASA (*Aggiornamiento Sistema d'Arma*) or 'updated weapon system' standard to enable the Starfighter to detect, track and shoot down low-level intruders began in February 1987 and, by 1993, 206 F-104S models had been so-modified. The original FIAT R2IG/H radar was replaced by FIAT R21G/M1 Setter with look-down/shoot-down capability and fire control system. Aspide 1A medium- to long-range, radar-guided air-to-air missiles, based on the Raytheon AIM-7E Sparrow AAM, replaced the Sparrows and fuselage rails were added for AIM-9L Sidewinder missiles. Improved IFF (Identification Friend or Foe), more modern internal electronic countermeasures (ECM) systems and an automatic pitch control computer were

Lockheed-built F-104F BB+365 (59-4999), one of thirty produced for the **Luftwaffe.** **(Lockheed)**

F-104S Starfighters of 37° Stormo 'Cesare Toschi' of the Aeronautica Militare Italiana *(AMI or Italian Air Force). (IAF)*

also fitted. Provision was also made for a reconnaissance camera pod. For air intercept sorties the F-104S typically carried an AIM-9L dogfight missile under the port wing, an Aspide 1A missile under the starboard wing and two wingtip tanks. In the fully loaded, but rarely used, interception configuration, the F-104S ASA carried four AIM-9 Sidewinders, two Aspides and two drop tanks. The introduction of the Tornado and, finally, the Eurofighter into the AMI inventory resulted in the gradual replacement of Starfighter units, the last being retired in May 2004.

All told, manufacturers in seven countries including Germany, Belgium, Italy and Holland produced 996 F-104G/RF-104G Starfighters. Altogether, Lockheed built 741 F-104s plus 48 co-produced by Lockheed and European consortium, 340 by Canadair, 444 by FIAT, 350 by Fokker, 50 by MBB, 210 by Messerschmitt, 207 by Mitsubishi and 188 by SABCA.

In 1963 the *Kongelige Norske Luftforsvaret* (KNL, Royal Norwegian Air Force) received sixteen Canadair-built F-104Gs as part of the American MAP programme. These were followed in 1965 by two RF-104s, which were rebuilt to F-104G standard, and in February 1966, an additional F-104G model. All of the F-104Gs were

modified to RF-104G standard for the all-weather fighter/interceptor (AWX) role. Surplus F-104Gs were dispatched to Turkey in June and July 1981. During the winter of 1973–74 *Skv334* re-formed at Bødo with eighteen ex-CAF CF-104s and four CF-104Ds. These aircraft were modified to carry Martin AGM-12C Bullpup air-to-surface missiles and operate in the anti-shipping role but the CF-104/-104Ds were finally phased out during the winter of 1982–83 and replaced by F-16A/B aircraft.

Deliveries to the *Elliniki Vassiliki Aeroporia* (Royal Hellenic Air Force) of Canadair/Lockheed-built F-104/TF-104Gs began in March–April 1964 under the terms of the Military Defense Assistance Programme (MAP). From December 1964 to February 1965 nineteen Canadair-built F-104Gs were obtained, which increased the number of F-104G/TF-104Gs supplied via MAP in 1964 to forty-four. In 1972 ten ex-Spanish AF F 104G/TF 104Gs were received. Wing Commander D. Jannes of the Greek Air Force who flew F-104s in the 1970s recalls the aircraft with affection:

The 'tube', as it was called was unique in taking 37% of the total lift from the fuselage and the rest from the wing and stabiliser! But it still flew! The

Two F-104G Starfighters of 5° Stormo 'Guiseppe Cenni' of the AMI or Italian Air Force. (IAF)

cockpit with the C-2 ejection seat was relatively comfortable, unless you tried to reach the stick shaker, undercarriage siren safety switches, UHF/IFF/Auto Pilot safety switches plus a few others which were buried somewhere down below you and which became, after 1973 and the installation of Martin Baker seats, just a memory! The forward view was excellent. You could see only the last 10cm of the pitot tube to remind you that you were in a plane and not in a flight simulator. The F-104 was particularly stable in close formation and all Starfighter pilots were experts in close formation flying – 9 planes in diamond formation occupied less space than a C-130! In 1½–2 hours (with external tanks of course) we would fly all over Greece at 450–500 knots at 200–300 feet, or even down to 10 feet!

The 'decisive' flight however was the air test. You went to the control room looking like 'Snake' Reeves (Lockheed's Chief Test Pilot and perhaps generally accepted as the best F-104 pilot). Young technicians looked at you in awe, the older ones in sympathy. After a little discussion on some details, things to note etc, you received a freshly painted,

F-104S of 4° Stormo 'Amendo d'Aosta' of the Aeronautica Militare Italiana *taking off.* (IAF)

fresh-from-inspection and clean (no tip tanks) F-104, ready for Mach 2.

After starting the J-79 and going through a swift process by communicating with the ground crew using all the fingers of your right hand, you were ready to taxi, all the time watching the engine gauges very carefully. You keep pushing the throttle and the squadron crew room became a blur. At the end of the runway, after going through the vital pre-take off checks and report to the tower 'canopy down – flaps down' the big moment came. You checked the engine and cleared for take-off, released the brakes and moved the throttle from minimum afterburner ... 3, 4, 5 seconds, max afterburner and from that moment on you forget anything else that you'd flown. 0–200 knots in 16 seconds with 15,800lbs of thrust one metre behind you and the first time, believe me, you don't even see the 1,000ft signs on either side of the runway. Then at 200 knots, you pulled back and then it was u/c up. Keep low down at 10 feet till the end of the runway where, at 370 knots, you pulled 2–3Gs until the artificial horizon unlocked (it does so at an 82° climb angle!). You then levelled off at 3–3,500 feet over the end of the runway, hoping that the CO didn't see you!

Two minutes later you were at 33,000ft (almost to the tropopause limit) over the sea off Zakinthos. After some stalls, flap checks etc., it was time for max afterburner. Time from M 1.1 to 1.4 was usually under a minute because in this region the air intakes didn't work too well, but then from M 1.4 to M2 took less than 30 seconds. You had to be careful not to exceed 121°C otherwise something would start melting back there! You then had to brake and slow down because fuel state was on 'Bingo'.

Instead of doing a 180 turn and returning to base at 35,000ft, you made a zoom climb at 20–25° in full afterburner until, say, 78,000ft, where you observed the certain roundness of the earth and the pitch black sky above. Keeping an eye on fuel, engine temperatures and the altimeter stuck at 45,000ft, you returned at 45–50,000ft via Andravida (an F-4E Phantom base 50 miles East of Araxos). From there you are direct onto finals on Runway 36 at Araxos. Forbidding yourself the luxury of an overshoot due to your low fuel state, you touched down on the tarmac with a big smile on your face. The technicians are looking back angrily and gauging how much paint has been stripped off the nose

cone and air intakes. Not bad after only 15 minutes of flight!

From 1981 to 1982 the *Elliniki Vassiliki Aeroporia* acquired ninety F-104G/RF-104G/TF-104Gs from Germany, and in May and July 1982 ten FIAT-built F-104Gs were acquired from the Royal Netherlands Air Force. Altogether, HAF operated 159 Starfighters. Greece lost sixteen pilots killed, the last remaining Starfighters being retired in spring 1993.

Beginning in November 1964, the Royal Danish Air Force received twenty-five Canadair-built F-104Gs and four Lockheed TF-104Gs to equip two squadrons at Aalbørg. In 1972–74 twenty-two ex-Canadian CF-104/CF-104Ds were transferred to Denmark. Starfighters were finally withdrawn from Danish service in April 1986 and, with the exception of four aircraft temporarily retained for target-towing duty, the Starfighters were retired from Danish service.

Under the terms of the Military Assistance Programme (MAP), Spain received eighteen C.8 and three CE.8 Starfighters (Canadair-built F-104Gs and Lockheed TF-104Gs respectively) and these were operated at Torrejón between February 1965 and 31 May 1972. These were replaced in service by two squadrons

Two F-104S of 4° Stormo 'Amendo d'Aosta' of the Aeronautica Militare Italiana *in flight.* (IAF)

of the F-4C Phantom II and in 1972 the Spanish Starfighters were returned to the USAF for transfer to Greece and Turkey. Spain was unique among the European operators of the Starfighter since it never lost an aircraft during their 17,060.35 hours of operational use. Spain joined NATO in 1982.

In 1965–66 The *Turk Hava Kuvvetleri* (THK, Turkish Air Force) received thirty-six new F-104G/TF-104G Starfighters under MAP. In 1972 eight F-104Gs and two RF-104Gs were transferred to Turkey from the Spanish Air Force. The THK obtained from Italy twenty F-104Gs and from December 1974 to mid-1976, forty F-104S interceptors. The F-104S replaced the last of the F-102A Delta Daggers in the fighter interceptor role. In 1976 Turkish Starfighters took part in the invasion of Cyprus. The THK acquired another fifty-three Starfighters from the Netherlands and from 1981 to 1983 seventeen F-104Gs were obtained from Belgium and thirteen

*Two F-104S of 3° Stormo 'Carlo Emanuele Buscaglia'
of the* Aeronautica Militare Italiana *in flight.* (IAF)

Fokker-built RF-104G D-8125 of the Royal Dutch Air Force. This Starfighter was acquired by the Turkish Air Force in November 1983. (RDAF)

Fiat-built F-104G D-6668 of the Royal Dutch Air Force. This Starfighter was acquired by the Greek Air Force in July 1982. (RDAF)

F-104G/TF-104Gs from Norway. By 1989 about another 148 F-104G/TF-104Gs were acquired from Germany. In 1965 the Canadian Government donated fifty CF-104/-104Ds. By 1986 Starfighters equipped thirteen *Filos* (squadrons) in the close support and air defence roles. From 1993 to 1994 the General Dynamics F-16 Fighting Falcon replaced the last Starfighters.

Pakistan, which remained an important ally of the United States through the Cold War, was the first non-NATO country to equip with the Starfighter. By September 1965, when hostilities broke out with its immediate neighbour India, the Pakistan Air Force (PAF) had only 150 aircraft, while the Indian Air Force (IAF) possessed approximately 900 aircraft. Twelve of the aircraft in the PAF inventory were Starfighters, the bulk of which were received in August 1961. These consisted of ten refurbished F-104As and two F-104Bs, all supplied under the US Military Defense Assistance Program (MAP). At PAF's request, all its F-104s were refitted with the M-61 gun. This and the more advanced J79-GE-II engine made the PAF F-104s unique – they had the gun and being the lightest of the F-104 series, therefore enjoyed the best thrust-to-weight ratio. The PAF Starfighters, which were each armed with two AIM-9B Sidewinder AAMs, were the first Mach 2-capable aircraft in Asia. Even in Europe at this time most countries were still flying subsonic aircraft. Even before its introduction to combat the Starfighter had gained such a reputation in the IAF that it was known as the 'badmash' ('scoundrel' or 'wicked one'). Many questioned Pakistan's ability to fly and maintain such a sophisticated aircraft as the F-104A/B, but PAF Starfighters were used throughout the wars with India in 1965 and in 1971.

In 1965 India had radar cover above 5,000ft, which made it virtually impossible for the Starfighter to achieve surprise, while subsonic aircraft operating under radar cover could easily defend themselves. The F-104s

would fly to 30,000ft and patrol the area near the disputed territory of Indian-held Kashmir. The first combat kill by a Mach 2 aircraft and the first missile kill for the PAF occurred on 6 September 1965 when a PAF F-104A shot down an IAF Mystère IV. Flying head-on into a formation of four lAF Mystère IVA aircraft that were attacking ground targets, Flight Lieutenant Aftab Alam Khan jettisoned his external fuel tanks and started to engage the Mystères as they turned into him. He aimed a Sidewinder at the nearest aircraft and heard the loud-pitched missile tone.

> The sight indicated that I was in range. With all the other requisite firing conditions met, I squeezed the trigger and kept it pressed. I waited, only to note that the missile had not fired. As I looked towards the left missile, I saw a big flash and the missile leaving the aircraft. The missile had taken, as stipulated in the manual, approximately 8/10ths of a second to fire after the trigger had been pressed but in combat, this seemed like an eternity. The flash of the missile blinded me for a few seconds. The radar controller, who was also monitoring the radio of the Mystères, immediately informed me that one Mystère had been shot down and that

TF-104Gs of WaSLw.10 in July 1971. (GAF)

*Jever-based F-104G 23+50 with EE Lightning
F.6 XR772/C of 11 Squadron RAF. (Tony Paxton)*

another had been damaged. It proved that the F-104 and the Sidewinder missile were an effective weapon system at low altitude.

During the 1965 war, the F-104s flew a total of 246 hours 45 minutes. Mostly, the missions flown were Air Defence and Air Superiority operations, but forty-two were at night against IAF Canberra B (I) 58s. The Starfighter's rudimentary AN/ASG-14T1 fire-control radar system could not illuminate small targets against ground clutter. The standard high-speed intercept tactic employed by PAF F-104 pilots was to approach their targets from below, with a typical height differential of 2,000–3,000ft, against a target they wished to acquire at a range of 10–15km. To pick up low-flying bombers on their scope, the F-104 pilots had to get down to about 300–500ft ASL (above sea level) to point their radars upward and clear of the ground clutter at the IAF bombers. On 21 September Squadron Leader (later ACM) Jamal A. Khan, flying an F-104A, intercepted an IAF Canberra B (I) 58 at about 33,000ft. He executed a perfect 'textbook' attack and shot it down with a Sidewinder near Fazilka, inside Pakistani territory. The bomber pilot ejected and was taken prisoner but the navigator, who could not eject, was killed in the action.

F-104G-LO- KF+134, which was built for the Luftwaffe *and was issued to* JaboG31, *crashed on 30 July 1969. The pilot,* Hauptmann *Achim Baumgardt, ejected safely.* (Lockheed)

(The British-built Canberra B (I) 58, unlike the Martin B-57, which the PAF used, had no ejection seat for the navigator.) This was the first kill achieved by an F-104 at night.

Although during the Indo–Pakistan War of 1971 the PAF scored a three-to-one kill ratio, destroying 102 IAF aircraft and losing 34 aircraft of its own, the war was only three days' old when East Pakistan fell. After just thirteen days, on 16 December, the war between India and Pakistan ended when Pakistan agreed to Indian demands for an unconditional surrender. The Indian victory was achieved with significant help from its ally the Soviet Union. Late in 1972 the PAF decided to phase the F-104 out of service after the inventory had been devastated as a result of a US Government arms embargo, which made it increasingly difficult to maintain a reasonable in-commission rate on the F-104A/Bs.

In Japanese service (1966–86), the Starfighter, or the *Eiko* (Glory), as it was known, equipped seven *Hiko-tais* (squadrons) of the *Nihon Koku Jieitai* (Japanese Air Self-Defence Force, or JASDF). Altogether, 210 F-104Js (and 20 F-104DJ operational trainers structurally similar to the F-104G but equipped as an all-weather interceptor) entered service with the JASDF. The first F-104DJ was assembled by Lockheed-Burbank and the remaining nineteen were reassembled in Japan by Mitsubishi

F-104A 56-804 of the Pakistan Air Force over the Himalayas. (PAF)

(fuselage and final assembly) and Kawasaki (main wing, tail and nose section). Outwardly almost identical to the F-104D, the F-104DJ differed in having a J79-1H1-11A turbojet of 10,000lb static thrust and 15,800lb with afterburner built under licence by Ishikawajima-Harima and an upward-firing ejection seat, while electronics and other items were compatible with those of the F-104J. All the two-seat trainers were delivered from July 1962 to January 1964. The first three F-104Js were produced and flight-tested by Lockheed, after which they were dismantled and shipped to Japan. A further twenty-nine were assembled by Mitsubishi Jukogyo KK (Mitsubishi Heavy Industries Ltd) at their Komaki plant in Japan and by Kawasaki, from Lockheed components, and 178 were built in two batches in Japan. Deliveries to the JASDF took place from March 1962 to March 1965. All F-104Js used operationally by the *Nihon Koku Jieitai* were optimized for the airborne interception role, normally carrying four AIM-9 Sidewinder AAMs and two underwing fuel tanks (no other stores were carried as the Japanese constitution bans weapons and aircraft with an offensive capability). On 12 June 1981 the JASDF reduced its Starfighter *Hiko-tais* from seven to four squadrons. Beginning in December 1981, the

F-104Js were progressively replaced by Mitsubishi-built F-15J/-15DJs and thirty-two F-104J/F-104DJs were acquired by the Nationalist Chinese Air Force on Taiwan. The last F-104Js in Japan were retired in March 1986 and a number were converted to drone aircraft.

Jordan acquired thirty-three F-104A/F-104Bs, which were formerly operated by the Nationalist Chinese Air Force in Taiwan until late in 1966. Initial deliveries to the *Al Quwwat Aljawwiya Almalakiya Alurduniya* (Royal Jordanian Air Force) were begun in the spring of 1967 but two days before the June Six-Day Arab-Israeli war the US removed the F-104s to Turkey. After the war ended the US refused to return the Starfighters to Jordan but after it appeared that King Hussein might turn to the Soviet Union and accept MiG-21s, the US relented and agreed to supply Jordan. Reissue of the (now refurbished) F-104As and four F-104Bs began in mid-1969. One of the Jordanian Starfighters saw combat during the failed coup against King Hussein in November 1972. The F-104/Bs were gradually replaced by the Northrop F-5E Tiger II and the last Starfighters were finally replaced by Dassault Mirage F1CJs in 1982–83. The survivors saw final service as airfield decoys.

Altogether, the Republic of China Air Force (RoCAF)

Three F-104S Starfighters of 5° Stormo 'Guiseppe Cenni' of the Aeronautica Militare Italiana *in flight.* (IAF)

of Taiwan received a total of 281 Starfighters, including 89 from the *Luftwaffe* and 27 ex-JASDF F-104Js under the 'ALISAN 9' project in 1978. The first two Starfighters were delivered in May 1960. From 1961 to 1962 and in 1964 a number of F/TF/RF-104Gs, fitted with Martin-Baker GQ7A ejection seats, were ordered. The first Canadair-built Starfighter for the RoCAF first flew on 7 October 1964 and the Gs were used to re-equip one squadron and also to replace the Sabres of two other squadrons. On 13 January 1967 twelve MiG-19s of the Chinese Air Force of the People's Liberation Army fought with four F-104Gs of the RoCAF over the disputed island of Quemoy. It resulted in the loss of an F-104G while one MiG-19 was claimed shot down. President Nixon's visit to Mainland China in 1978 resulted in much closer ties with the United States, while the introduction of more modern aircraft to Taiwan was delayed for fear of upsetting the Communist regime. As a result, Taiwan broke off diplomatic relations

F-104S ASA 9-39 of 9° Stormo 'Francesco Baracca' of the Aeronautica Militare Italiana *at RAF Coltishall in the summer of 2000.* (Author)

with the US and it was forced to source its Starfighters from further afield. They came not just from NATO nations, but also from Japan and Taiwan was able to replace its ageing F-100A Super Sabres with Starfighter aircraft. From 1996 to 1997 all remaining Starfighter units were either re-equipped with the General Dynamics F-16A/B Fighting Falcon or the Dassault Mirage 2000-5.

F-104S ASA 9-33 of 9° Stormo 'Francesco Baracca' of the Aeronautica Militare Italiana *at RAF Coltishall in the summer of 2000. (Author)*

Wing Commander D. Jannes of the Greek Air Force sums up the Starfighter's colourful history.

With the F-104 you had a love hate relationship, nothing mid way. Very few people came to hate it. For most, the F-104 had a special place in their hearts, no matter what they came to fly later – even the F-15. At 0.9 Mach, initial climb rate was 50,000ft/minute. Time from brakes release to 35,000ft was less than 3 minutes! Well, the F-15 in the meantime would have reached 99,000ft but we're talking about a 1954 design and the first flight of the G-model was in 1960 when the F-15 didn't exist, not even as a low voltage circuit in the memories of the McDonnell Douglas computers! Look, it didn't mean that the F-104 is the best plane. Certainly, aircraft like the F-16, F-18 and Mirage 2000 could do circles around an F-104. However, an F-16 pilot who would have reached 80–85% of the capabilities of his jet (the maximum figure for the average pilot) would make a minimum effort by comparison to that of an F-104 pilot and that's the key point in the philosophy behind the F-104. The pilot who flies the F-16 at 90% of its limits will come back thrilled. The pilot who approached the same figure in the F-104 would come back really shaken, having done the Perfect Flight.

David L. Bashow, a very experienced CF-104 pilot in the Canadian Air Force, concludes:

The F-104 used to be the hottest fighter for so many years and she could truly be flown high, wide and handsome. Some of her shortcomings were doubtless the result of inexperience on the part of those that designed and rested her and the political pressure that was exerted in the early years. In the hands of a capable pilot the Starfighter could chalk up respectable gunnery scores on towed targets. It was a good, stable, weapons platform and handled well under instrument flying conditions. Accidents happened, but these never made us professionals dislike the Starfighter. One thing was certain; many genuine tears were shed into many a beer when the old gal's wheels were chocked and her big turbine wound down for the last time.

Thanks for the memories, Kelly Johnson.

F-104S ASAs of 9° Stormo 'Francesco Baracca' of the Aeronautica Militare Italiana *taxi out at RAF Coltishall in the summer of 2000.* (Author)

LOCKHEED F-104
STARFIGHTER
Interceptor/ Strike/ Reconnaissance Fighter

F-104G Starfighter
(FX52)
31 Smaldeel
Belgische Luftmacht / Force Aerienne Belge.

**CF-104D Starfighter
(N104RB)**
Civilian display team.
Ex Royal Canadian Air Force.

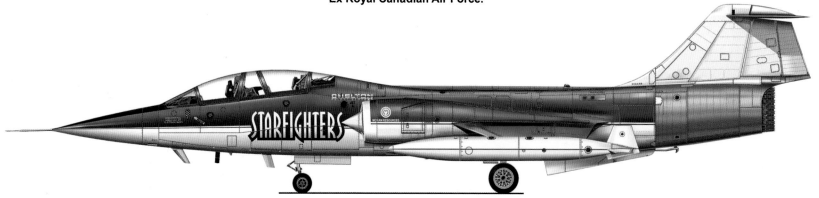

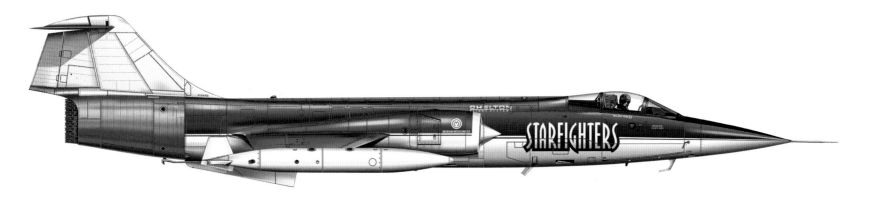

**CF-104 Starfighter
(N104RD)**
Civilian display team.
Ex Royal Canadian Air Force.

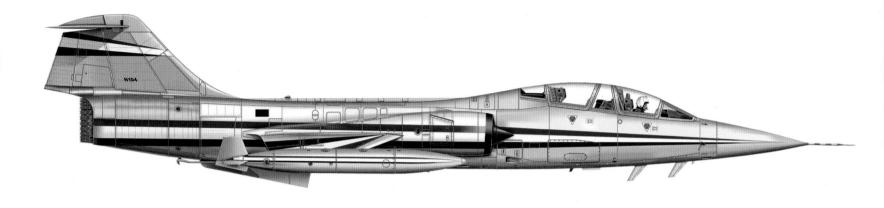

CF-104D Starfighter
(N104)
Civilian display.
Ex Royal Canadian Air Force.

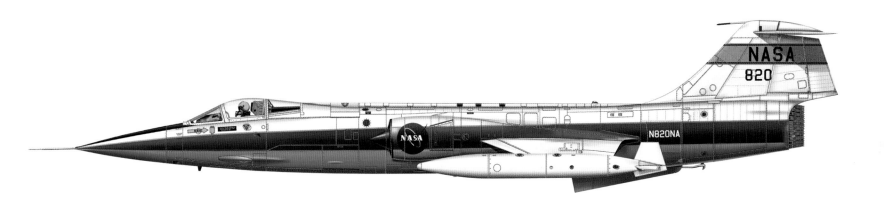

**F-104A/G Starfighter
(N820NA)**
NASA

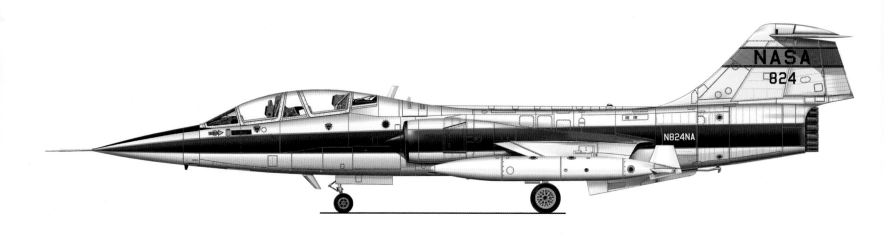

**TF-104G Starfighter
(N824NA)**
NASA

CF-104 Starfighter
(104838)
No. 439 Squadron
Royal Canadian Air Force.

F-104S ASA Starfighter
(MM6827)
311° Gruppo
Reparto Sperimentale Volo (Test Wing)
Aeronautica Militare Italiana

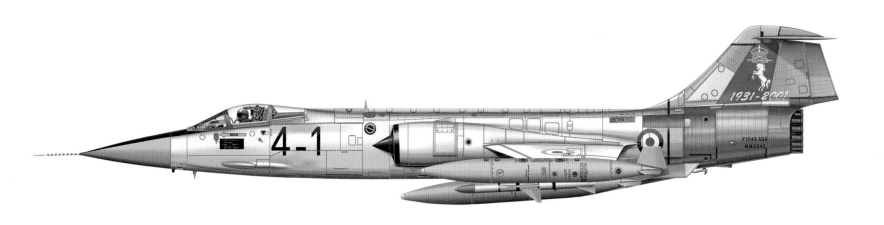

**F-104S ASA Starfighter
(MM6943)**
9° Gruppo, 4° Stormo
Aeronautica Militare Italiana

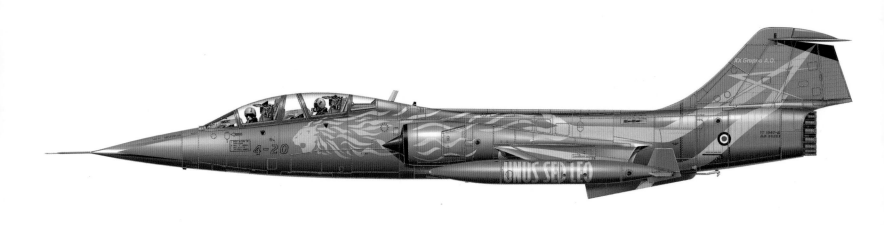

TF-104G-M Starfighter
(MM54253)
20° Gruppo
Aeronautica Militare Italiana

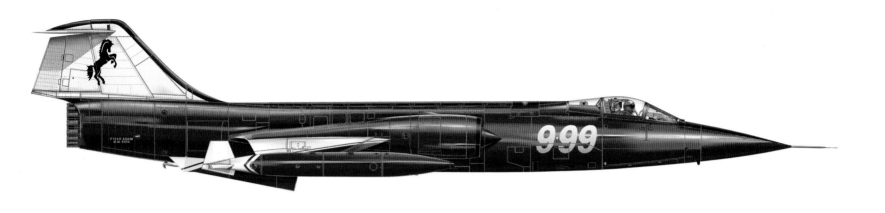

F-104S ASA-M Starfighter
(MM6930)
9° Gruppo, 4° Stormo
Aeronautica Militare Italiana

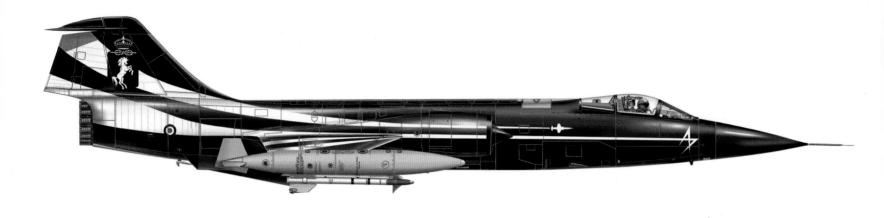

F-104S ASA-M Starfighter
(MM6873)
9° Gruppo, 4° Stormo
Aeronautica Militare Italiana

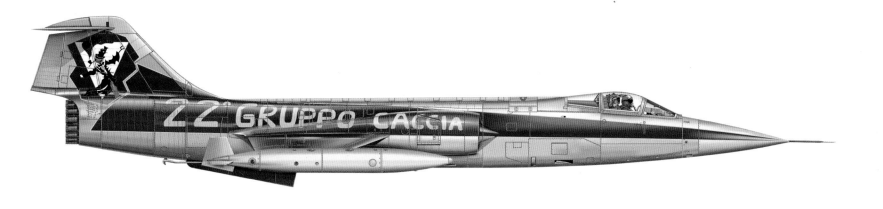

F-104G Starfighter
(MM6529)
22° Gruppo, 51° Stormo
Aeronautica Militare Italiana

F-104G Starfighter
(MM6579)
28° Gruppo, 3° Stormo
Aeronautica Militare Italiana

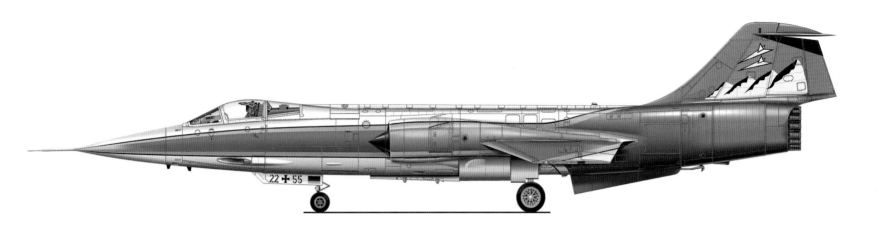

F-104G Starfighter
(22+55)
Jagdbombergeschwader 34 (JBG 34)
Luftwaffe.

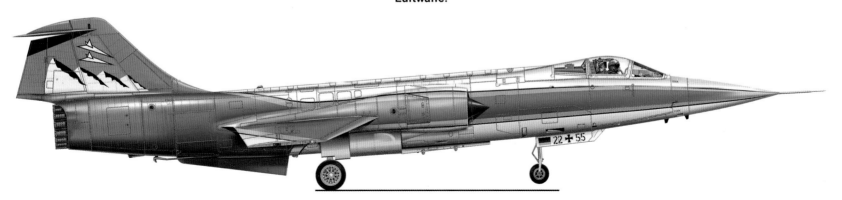

F-104G Starfighter
(26+72)
Marinefliegergeschwader 2 (MFG 2)
Marineflieger

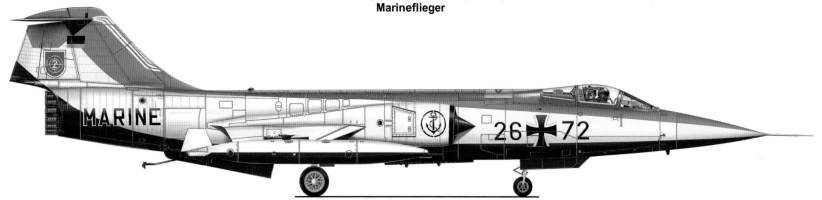